I0840608

1.

Pain

The Introduction

I didn't know much about my interest at four or five years old. However, I know that I loved music. It took me out of what I didn't understand.. It took me from what I later come to understand as pain. I could feel music as if the artist was there singing to me. I remember the times moma would smile she'd be singing, so I smiled and sang with her. Then came my introduction to pain.

I was maybe 4 or 5 years old when I heard daddy fussing at mom about dinner. He was tired of chicken and today we were having chicken and noodles again. Mattie I'm getting sick and tired of eating damn chicken. Every damn time I turn around I come home to you cooking chicken. You cook another chicken I'm gone cluck. I promise you this was his 26th time saying it because I kept count. I wanted to know how many times you had to eat chicken to cluck. I wanted to avoid the mishap of clucking like a chicken. My mother proceeded to cook as if he didn't say a word. I know she heard him because my sister Sadie, and I were all the way upstairs preparing to make moma smile. Sadie was kinda lucky because she was hearing impaired so she couldn't hear the harshness in daddy's voice. I knew when daddy talk like that momma don't look right. Her face didn't have that light like when she'd listen to music. It's like her favorite songs gave her life. I had to do something to help, so Sadie and I went in my parents room.

 There was my parents clock radio that played music. If I could find the right song I could make moma smile. Then daddy will think shes pretty and forget about chicken for the 26th time... I never found that perfect song.

Chapter 1

The Source

The night came and I didn't like sharing a room with Sadie because she wet the bed. That was the only problem I had with Sadie. She was my closest friend. The next morning I was up before everyone. I would always get up before everyone. I wanted to see if I could find some cereal, toast... Something to eat! Nope, nothing. Not even the food pantries finest toasted flakes. My stomach was growling louder than the old floor squeaked as I ran upstairs. Made it to my room, and Sadie was sound asleep. Grabbed my only two dolls, sat on my make believe throne at the top of the stairs, and proceeded to play away the hunger pains. As I began to take my throne I heard my dad's voice. This was very odd because it's 9am. He's gone for work by six. "Mattie, what time that clock got?" "Its 9:02." Mattie replied. Not acknowledging him as her husband, or stating his name. Just a simple reply as if she was his employee. "I'm gonna kill CiCi dumb ass.

She was the last one messing with this clock trying to turn on the radio. By that time I think all the blood in my body started to boil. I was sweating, hot like fire with terror running thru. I knew that tone didn't mean anything nice. Just as soon as I decided to run. I was frozen in my footsteps by the sound of my parents bedroom door lunging open. Before I could respond to daddy calling my name, his fist met the side of my head, and my head met the corner of the wall. Dazed, and feeling the warmth of my blood run down my face. I was confused. Misunderstood. A child only going on five years old. My thoughts were cut short to darkness as I received another blow to the head. The darkness channelled me back to my throne.

There I was getting my feet washed by a villager showing gratitude. The darkness channelled me into survival mode. Taking me to a safe place of resistance from physical, and emotional pain. I woke up to find myself in the bathtub. The water running on my feet as my mother cleaned blood from my face, hands, and body. I looked at her face. The place where I once saw life was gone. All was left were tears, and the blank stare of sorrow. I didn't want her to feel bad, so I complimented her beauty.

For years to come the face became regular. My blackout survival tactic became routine before I could write my name. I could channel my mind into survival mode. My only defense mechanism against physical pain. Then carry on, and don't run your mouth. I learned at an early age you take it, and you shake it. No matter how much it hurts. I was able to escape the pain. I'm still not sure if I took the time to address the hurt. Hell, nobody cared outside of myself. No one saw how much hurt I carried. I was invisible.

Chapter two

The next morning I remember waking up empty. My head was pounding something terrible. My right eye was swollen, and vision blurry. I didn't know what to do or how to feel. I looked out my window, then cried myself back to sleep. I didn't want to get up. Hell, I didn't want to feel again. I was only four years old when hopelessness introduced itself into my life.

I finally decided to get up out of bed. I was afraid of making too much noise, so I tipped toed down the stairs, to the kitchen. There has to be something for me to eat. I was starving by this time. I stayed in my room for two days without food. Nobody in the house checked for me. The house carried on as usual for those two days. I felt like I didn't exist. My mom would open the door, and call my name. Once I'd respond she'd go on her way. My father never did.

When I got to the kitchen I was so happy to see a loaf of bread. I put four pieces in the toaster, spread some butter on them, little sugar, and a little bit of cinnamon. I'm not even sure if I took the time to chew. I was starving! Drank a glass of water in gulps, then quickly cleaned up my mess. I prayed while walking up the stairs. I prayed that I didn't get beat for eating the bread. I was so thirsty, and hungry. I simply couldn't take it anymore. I sat on my bed, and took a look out the window. Before long I was crying my eyes out. That was the first time I questioned why was I born. It sure as hell wasn't the last time, I asked myself that question. I felt worthless, and hopelessness at the same time. Looking out the window, only to imagine being elsewhere. To be anywhere outside of the place I called home.

Chapter Three

The Start

It's time to start kindergarten. I barely knew how to write my name. You see in my household it wasn't much time for nurturing and building fundamentals. Pop's had to put food on the table, clothes on our backs, as well as keep the lights and heat on. Mama was often not well, so who had time to teach ABC's. I knew my first day of school wasn't going to be easy. I tried my best, but was often distracted. After awhile words would run together, or certain words would jump out at me. Then I'd read an entire chapter, and have no clue what I just read. I could sense the teachers frustration with me asking for help. It was embarrassing to see them roll their eyes in their heads. Followed by the long sigh of "what is it now Miss Green?" Then the class would burst into laughter at my expense. After while I stopped asking for help.

By the time spring break came around I didn't show any progress. It was now time for school officials to speak with my parents. Shit! The minute I hand over this note to mama it's over!

It's mid April and daddy was working less. When I arrived home with this note that almost made me piss myself on the way; pop's was there. He's been home early lately these days. I didn't hesitate going straight to mama with my note. I knew better than to poke the bull. I then proceeded to my spot on the stairs, no longer my pretend throne to take a seat. I heard my mom tell dad "Al, we gotta go up to the school. They say CiCi having some trouble with her learning." There was a slight pause. Then pop's replied. "That's because she dumber than a jackass!" I heard the words, but I felt them like a blow to the face as they leaped out of my father's mouth. He proceeded to say. "That child act like she don't understand english. She look you dead in your face and don't understand nothing you say.

 When it's time to run her mouth or take some shit apart and put it back together, you can't stop her ass. That girl ain't all there Mattie I tell ya!" Maybe I was a dummy. My dumb ass thought the top of the stairs was my thrown. I'm not supposed to run my mouth about family business. Family business was all i knew, so I didn't have friends outside of my sister Sadie. I didn't have anything to talk about with friends. They talked about family trips, nights at the movies with their parents, family night... What the hell is family night? I was the quiet loner who didn't fit in. At home I was the clueless busy body. I wanted to know how stuff worked so I took stuff apart. Would often talk too much. Most times it was out of term. I'd see one of my sister's boyfriends with another woman.

 Thanksgiving dinner roll around, Tyrone come through the door my little butt was gonna announce across the room who I saw Tyrone with. As well as the when and where. Maybe I was a dummy... Too much thinking! I'm gonna lay my dumb ass down, and take my mind away with some music. As I laid in bed my mom slowly crept through my door. Her big brown eyes, and beautiful textured brownish red hair were the first things I noticed as she stuck her head in the door. She entered slowly with her favorite big green sundress with white pinstripes. I remember her dress flowing like an angel as she stood next to the vent when the furnace clicked on.. "Cici what's going on at school?" I don't know ma. I try my best, but I think the teachers get tired of me asking for help." Well, do you talk to any of the other children? Do you have any friends?" No. They think I'm weird. They mostly talk about me than to me. I'm scared to say anything because I might say too much. I told mama. I don't want to get in trouble, or say the wrong thing. I go to school keep my mouth shut. Just like I'm told. "Try talking about the things you like. When someone talks to you try to show some expression. Smile back when someone smile at you.

 You look so lost all the time Cici." She just don't know most of the time I am. I'm not about to tell her though. That would only make her sad, so I simply said; I will try to fit in more mama. I told myself from then on I was gonna be normal like everyone else. I'll do as I'm told and what I see. I'll figure it out later when I'm alone and it's cool to be me.

The school is now past its third attempt to get my parents in for a meeting. Now we're scheduled for a home visit. My father was pissed! He knocked me to the floor until he was no longer frustrated. He didn't like people coming by the house. He didn't like our house. It wasn't always clean, and some of the furniture was falling apart. Not to mention my payless Eastland loafers had holes in the sole. I knew better than to tell my father I needed shoes. He was worked up enough about the bills. He's home all the time now that the factory he worked for closed down. I was not about to add me needing shoes to his stress.

I got an old corn flake box, cut the cardboard in the exact pattern as the sole of my shoe. I then wrapped it with the plastic wrap. Next I covered them in duct tape, and wrapped them snug with aluminum foil. Boom! Shoe inserts! I did my best to not be a nuisance for my parents, and now this damn school wants to come to my house. I remember waiting for my parents to fall asleep that night. Soon as they went to bed I cleaned the house from top to bottom. I didn't want my parents upset. Making sure no one worried about the house not being up to parr. I didn't sleep at all that night. I literally worked until the sun started to rise. The next morning my daddy was so proud of me. It was an expression I rarely got a chance to see. One I would never forget. I remembered facial expressions so I knew how to look normal and not lost or empty. So I most definitely noticed the expression of gratitude on his face. "Girl you cleaned this house all by yourself?" Pop's asked me. Yes I did daddy! With my chest all poked out.

"You did a good job baby girl." Finally! I did something right! I'm useful, so I'm worthy! Sadie shot her regular. Not a care for the world she didn't understand. Her being developmentally handicapped she spent a lot of time at special schools, and with different types of social workers from school. She was bussed outside the city for special education. Our district didn't offer the services she needed, so she attended a school in Mayfield. Mornings, and bedtime is when I saw Sadie the most. She would save her snacks from school, so we'd have something in the morning to eat just in case there was no food in the house. Lance cookies and cakes baby! Please believe me when I tell you I love cookies. I could eat them all day because it was the cookies fault I was a busy body pops would say. Not mine. I had an excuse for being hyperactive. Plus they are so yummy! Almost Home and Archway were my favorite. She made sure I had some everyday. I made sure nobody fucked with her everyday. Even if it meant sacrificing myself. We signed good morning to each other everyday. She'd hand me a honey bun, and Lance sandwich cookies. Then dart out to her bus stop. Sadie was funny like that. I headed out a little frustrated. It was raining out, and I was tired of the rain seeping through my inserts as I walked to school. I would go most of the school day with my feet soaked. Then as the day would progress they would start smelling foul.

That's how I earned the name funky CiCi in school. Pissed about my shoes. I walk out the door, and my mom reminds me to swing my arms as I walk. She said I walk too stiff and tight. Swing my arms? I thought to myself. I need shoes and I'm hungry! Swing my damn arms for what? Whatever! Off I went. Walking to school looking like a damn marching robot. I didn't care. I simply wanted to make it through another day of torture. I did better figuring assignments out on my own with my text book than I did in the classroom. Still I went everyday. By end of day I was simply grateful of making it through another day.

I knew when I saw the unfamiliar car in the driveway that someone from my school was still there. Soon as I walked through the door my mom had that fake it's all good look plastered across her face. I actually smelled food cooking. And pop's... Well pops was looking restless, ready for this woman to get out of his house. His demeanor was chill, but his eyes looked at this pretty lady smelling like roses as if she was the devil. I heard words like evaluation needed, learning disabilities, dyslexia, autism, lack of comprehension. Then I heard genius problem solver, great attention to certain details of her interest, and the ability to make something out of any material she is given. " I believe after the proper evaluation, and we know truly what's going on and proper nourishment Cierra can grow to become something great." I remember thinking damn! I can be something great? I've never heard someone speak of me that way. Then it dawned on me. She didn't know me.

My mother didn't hear anything the woman said outside of proper nourishment. Because her response was "Cierra always has proper nourishment. She probably didn't eat enough that day." Hell, I can't recall a day outside the holidays when I had enough to eat. As Mrs. Mendoza made her exit I could feel the heat coming from my father all the way from the kitchen. When I looked towards him sure enough he was looking at me with ass whooping on his mind. Soon as the door closed daddy was in my face. "So you at school telling people we don't have food?" I never got to respond because I was cut off by his fist knocking me upside the head. After the third blow to the head I let my mind go black. When I go black I can't feel him hitting me, but It doesn't hurt. I can project myself anywhere, and be anything... Or anyone. I remember picturing myself as Mr. T. I was kicking my dad's ass! Telling him "stop hitting people fool! I pity the fool." I giggled thinking about it. That's when the blows got harder.

I didn't go to school a whole week after because my butt and legs were too sore to walk. I don't remember talking, or telling anyone about the pain I was in. I completely shut myself off. I didn't express a single emotion. Yet I couldn't stop the tears falling from my eyes. I woke up everyday to cry. I ended my day with tears. All because I couldn't tell a soul how I was feeling. I didn't know how. Maybe when I'm older I will understand. I'll see what the next school year has to offer. I clearly blew this year.

Chapter four

The next school year didn't bring much progress. All I knew at this point was survival. I was a child, and I wanted to be an adult. I wanted out... Out of the life I was living. I had no life. I didn't have friends. I sat around a bunch of adults complaining all the time. About any and everything they could think of.

We didn't travel much, but we'd visit family from time to time. We'd visit my dad's side of the family most. I love them, but at the same time can't stand some of their ways. Some of the elders on my dad's side lacked compassion, and understanding. Some of them were extremely judgemental. My aunt Dessy, Beaty, and Uncle Moe lived in one duplex home. When we would visit for the holidays it would be family hanging out everywhere. I'm talking wall to wall Greens.

 Family from right here at home, St. Louis, Detroit, Chicago, Mississippi, and Alabama. My aunts and my uncle would cook up several different feast. I'm talking the works! From turkey, dressing, ham, fried chicken, candy yams, greens, mac & cheese, black eyed peas, cornbread, chitterlings, and a boat load of sweets! I loved me some aunt Betty German Chocolate cake. I simply didn't care for her and aunt Daisy's attitude towards my mom and family.

It was July fourth, and it had to be at least 100 degrees outside. I knew we were spending the holiday with my dad's family. I heard him on the phone with my uncles from St. Louis earlier that day. They were talking about crown royale, and Uncle Moe "stankin ass" pipe. Plus I had a new outfit. Mom and pop's always bought me a new outfit when it was time to visit the jury... I mean family. I remember being told a million times not to mess up the outfit before we arrived. I thought to myself who cares! They don't like us anyway. Still, I didn't get dirty. I knew better than that.

Once we arrived you could hear the blues blaring thru the door. They were playing Muddy Waters Hoochie Coochie Man. You could smell food in the air as we walked thru the door. Along with Virginia Slims, Newports, Salems, Kools, liquor, beer, feet, and sweat.

"Their goal with that wife and child of his" Aunt Beaty yelled. Then she leaned in to Aunt Dessy, and whispered. "Cici starting to look old and tired just like Mattie ass." They both chuckled, but I didn't see the punch line. That was one towards the person I loved the most. I don't go past two times. I'm very protective of the few I love. I think now because I've never felt protected by the people that were supposed to love me. I knew my mother's story. I knew what she endured on a daily basis. I know what she sacrificed to survive. She gave up herself to be able to provide for us...me. So I didn't take kindly to anyone trying to downplay the woman she was.

It's now winding down, the men, and children have been served. Now the ladies were eating. I sat next to my mom in case she needed my help. On the opposite side was Aunt Beaty and Aunt Dessy. My mother had suffered a mild stroke and had cardiovascular issues. Because of this her hands would shake sometimes. We were all eating when i noticed mama was spilling food on her shirt. Not much, but enough for me to notice. I guess I wasn't the only one noticed. Before I could even ask mama if she needed help Aunt Beaty blurted out. "Damn! Mattie ass can't even get the food in her mouth!" Everyone found this to be funny for some reason. Not me though! Bitch that's two! Remember I don't go past two. You big fat bitch! You always have something to say about my mother. I'm tired of you talking about my damn mother! She was smoking hot now! I've never seen a moor turn red but Auntie was red as a beat! She was pissed!

"You little ugly duckling who you think your nappy head ass talking to?" She asked me through clenched teeth. I'm talking to you! You big black walrus! I'm not my mother. I will beat the shit out of you! If you don't like my mother don't invite her over. I don't think Auntie understood what I was carrying internally. If she did she would've noticed my clenched fists, the pulsating in my temples, the tapping of my foot. I had something I wanted to deliver, and it wasn't any shit smelling roses. It was a long overdue ass whooping. I hated people that hit to express themselves when angry. But mostly I hated the Bullies, and belittling of people. Aunt Betty was a mean old bully! I reached back to my ankles, and tried to knock her head clean off her shoulders. I hit her just like daddy would hit me. Her wig flew across the room, and the entire house was silent for a moment.

My mother knew beat down was brewing within me. She screamed my name. "Cierra Green! Come with now chile!" She marched my little grown butt across the hall to Uncle Moe's house. My dad and his brothers were there drinking crown royal and smoking cigars. Aunt Betty was hot on our heels. The minute we walked in my mother started to speak. Beaty threw her hand out for my mom to shut up. I then balled my fist, and punched the shit out of Beauty ass again. My mother was speaking to her husband about her child. Beaty had no place in the conversation yet. I was so afraid when I realized what I've done. I was crying hysterically, and filled with emotions that I couldn't control, and afraid of them just the same. Before my father could tear my butt a new one I told him the truth. The truth came as if I were screaming the words through a bullhorn. I hate coming over here! All they do is sit and make fun of my mother. They call me ugly all the time, and call us broke. We come over to be their punchline. I'm tired of them. I hate the way they pick on my mother! For the first time I think he heard me. He told me to sit next to him. He then sent Aunt Beaty ass back the same way she came. Hot! My mom sat with us. He leaned over towards me, and gave me a pound. "Always take care of ya people Cici. You a strong little girl, but you can't go around knocking the shit out my sister's. Remember your respect girl." We both smiled, and I replied heard. That was that last time for many years to come I celebrated a holiday with the Green side of the family. Aunt Beaty didn't talk to me again until I was thirty five.

Chapter five

She a big girl now

Shit, I'm in Jr high school now. Still, without friends, but no one picked on me anymore. No longer was I a target for bullies. I couldn't protect myself at home due to my loyalty respect and fear. At school it was a different story. I was older, bigger, and stronger. I can protect myself in this setting. Never bothered anyone or treated anyone bad. Simply kept to myself and mind my own business. Almost always ready to give anyone who stepped to me all that I was carrying. If someone did something as simple as popping my bra strap. I would kick ass! I'd beat you in one inch of your life. I would suppress every blow verbally, and physically given by my father. Any form of abuse I was given I blocked it. This way of thinking only made my emotions spill everywhere. When time came to express myself I failed. I had so much bottled up expression became frustration for those who didn't understand. I released all that I was carrying when someone tried to hurt me.

By this time I started having blackouts. Not the kind where shit goes black like you're asleep. The kind where you're somewhere totally different, with different people in different situations. Often times it would be in certain situations where I couldn't protect or defend myself. By the time it was all said, and done I'd have no clue of the damage. I have to remember where I am and usually can't tell you anything that happened in between. Only that I hurt someone who was trying to hurt me. Period. This made communication hard, and I had no idea of self worth. I was becoming a teenager lacking self worth. Two things I knew for sure though was how to survive during tough time. Also how to be useful. Lets see how useful I'd be in a new school, with new people. I was going to Jr High! This was my opportunity to start fresh. Be different, and maybe make some friends.

I didn't do a damn thing in Jr high school. I did however get the guts to try out for the volleyball, and field hockey team. I made both teams. I was actually extremely good at both. I Just couldn't maintain the grades to stay on the team. No matter what though I continued showing up every day, as well as doing my best. My mind simply couldn't get it right. I would often have trouble understanding the lessons as they were taught. Also, no one at home was concerned enough to help me. Everyone was too busy trying to survive. By this time we all were. Sadie suffered from a hearing impairment with low functionality. You would never know this because we were taught if nothing else how to act. Or simply shut the hell up. Sadie knew shit wasn't right, so she stopped being at home. She'd stay with her boyfriend majority of the time. Our home was the house of horrors we couldn't tell anyone about. Not even about the demon that touched us at night. We were trained to say nothing, own nothing and don't embarrass the family. I was never comfortable with any of it. Hell, I wasn't comfortable with myself. Everyday I was missing Sadie something terrible, but I didn't have time to. There was work to do. We had a house full! My oldest sister "Lil" Mattie moved back home with two infants, and my second oldest sister Chelsea split from her husband and left her four children for my parents to finish raising. Yeah go figure! I could only Imagine having enough to eat now. Hell, sometimes we didn't have soap. My brother Curtis has never shown up for life. He has been on drugs for as long as I can remember. He'd speak to me, and I could see the lack of esteem in his eyes. Followed by the thoughts of inadequacy in his head. I could also see the shame in him from carrying all this baggage. His addiction to crack cocaine was evident, and undeniably his weakness. He was a "sucka" to me. Someone who compromises themselves for a moments gratification...sucka. He turned to humiliating himself on drugs making daddy an even more bitter person. This left me feeling like I had to be productive to pops in some kind of way. At least enough to where I don't get my ass kicked. I felt I had to be one less disappointment.

I wasn't productive at school, but I was for damn sure was productive at home. By my 8th grade year Big Mattie had began to show major signs of depression. She stopped talking, or showing any emotion. One day she woke up, and she was no longer full of life. She got up, drank coffee, and sat in a chair all day. I made the mistake of telling her about the demon touching me and Sadie at night, when her and my dad would be away, or asleep. The topic was quickly moved to the family business vault. I was told that I was exaggerating, and to never repeat that shit again. I knew the consequences, so I kept my mouth shut. I'm not sure Big Mattie handled it well. She shut down and shut me out after. So now it's me holding it down. Now I'm responsible for the whole damn house. I would come home from school, change my niece and nephew diaper, clean the house, find something to make for dinner, laundry, homework, get our clothes ready for school the next day, and maybe catch an episode of What's Happening or The Cosby Show if I wasn't too tired. This was my routine, and where I excelled. It made me feel useful. I was finally good at something. Long as I'm useful I'm tolerated. If they tolerated me, they loved me.

Beat from my daily routine I decided to retire to my room with my headphones. Soon as I opened my door standing there in the mirror, was my sister Chelsea. She was wearing a stone washed jean dress, cowboy riding boots, and fishnet stockings. She was getting ready for a date. I remember staring at her thinking how pretty she was. Wishing I looked and dressed like her. I was a funny looking' chick with a unibrow flat butt and hair that won't grow. Who was I fooling? Pretty wasn't in the cards for this ugly duckling. After awhile I guess she got annoyed with me staring at her. Chelsea asked what was my ugly ass looking at? She didn't hesitate to tell me how weird I was, nor forget to ask the famous "what the fuck is was wrong with you" question. I guess it never dawned on the rocket scientists who raised me to seek help. They couldn't see me, but I sure as hell saw them.

I simply replied I don't know and dove in bed. I mean if she didn't want me to look at her get out my room. Bad enough because of her kids I'm back sharing my room, and barely eating. Who was I kidding? I wasn't allowed an opinion, emotions, or a voice. I was simply here. No structure, no purpose. All I knew was how to be useful, serve others, and survive. That's how you get along with the people you love, and they love you back... So I thought.

I'm to the point I hate coming home. It's always something to be done. I never got a chance to explore my own interest. There was always some shit to do! I'm babysitting everyday all day. I had Lil Mattie kids with me everywhere I went. I had peanut on my hip, and winky in hand. I walked everywhere I had to go with these two kids. I loved, and protected them both with everything I had. I simply wanted time for myself once, and awhile. I quickly got over it. There was no need to dwell on what would never happen.

I was completely beat by end of day. I cleaned the house from top to bottom. Took care of all the laundry down to the table clothes. There wasn't a dirty item in the house once I got done.

After doing all the housework I'd make dinner for an army of Greens. By the time the kids, and I got done eating, my energy was completely drained! I ran a bath for them, then one for myself. It was lights out for us at 7pm. I didn't fit in at home. Talking to anyone outside of Peanut, and Winky wasn't a big deal to me. I'd come in walk past my entire family, and go to my room. They only told me how much I got on their nerves, or what I did wrong anyway. I didn't really have a desire to talk to anyone. I kept most of my feelings to myself. My solitude was, and still is my comfort zone. Especially after interacting with people. Most people are superficial, and judgemental. Those type of people drain my spirit.

Laying in bed with my feet pulsating from too small shoes. I'm not sure if anyone noticed I'd outgrown my shoes. I was too afraid to say something, and as a result. I began to feel hopeless.

I looked out the window, and wished I was a Huxtable. If only I was a kid on The Cosby Show. I closed my heavy eyes. Then slowly drifted off to sleep. Hoping I'd wake up, and this life was a bad dream.

Chapter six

The next morning I got up super early. I didn't have to babysit, and mama said we were going to visit "grampie" today. Grampie was my grandfather. My mother's father was the coolest grandpa on the planet. I enjoyed visiting, and spending time with him. Who am I kidding I loved it! He was hilarious. Gramp lived in a multi unit home filled with the loving part of my family. Here I wasn't invisible. My Aunt Sherry, and her three children lived with grampie. Aunt Lenora lived upstairs with her four children. It was a whole lot of family living in one house. My big cousins were the coolest on the planet. They stuck together, and always supported each other. It was all love all the time over there.

Pops slowly pulled our two door, 1982 Buick Regal in the driveway. My cousin Ricky, and half the neighborhood kids were in the yard. Pops did his usual fussing telling kids to move, so he could park. They were busy having a wrestling match in the backyard. It must've been half the street in their backyard. I remember thinking to myself soon as Aunt Sherry come home she's cussing Ricky out! She told him several times stop having all the neighborhood kids in the yard. She also told him about using her aluminum foil to make wrestling belts. This fool had three of Reynolds Wrap finest championship belts hanging on the fence.

Aunt Sherry gonna kick your ass! "Shut up Woodstock!" Ricky replied, laughing, while giving me a high five. That was the rude nickname my cousin Stan gave me. He was my Aunt Lenora's oldest son. I earned this nickname because my hair would stick up all over the place. Something like Woodstock the little yellow bird with Snoopy. We laughed, and I went inside. Grampie was sitting in his brown leather recliner. He would always greet me with a big smile, so I smiled back. "Hey baby girl! Come give gramp a hug." I gave him the tightest hug, followed by a kiss on the cheek. Hey grampie! I know you got some watermelon. Gramp always had a ripe watermelon in the fridge. Seemed as if he'd find the best ones. Hardly any seeds, and juicy.

"I sure do. Go in there, and cut us a piece." He didn't have to tell me twice! Aunt Sherry had Oreos in the cookie jar on the kitchen counter. I have a major thing for cookies, so I helped myself to about six, or seven. Gave grampie his watermelon, and munched my cookies while heading to the front porch. Cousin Stacy, and Shellie were chilling on the porch. Aunt Lenora's second oldest, and youngest. They were hanging out with their friends doing each other's hair, while Scott La Rock pumped through the boombox speakers. I hit the porch, and cousin Stacy started flagging me. That's the signal for me to give my ear to her. She had something to say for my ears only. That was one of many things I loved about them. They talked to you. Not about you. Especially with other people. I didn't receive encouragement, inspiration, or hardly any type nurturing outside of my Tuscora family. I often got criticized, belittled, or my ass kicked at home. I would often feel bad. Just like the bad things said to, and about me on a regular basis. So, you know it was extremely refreshing to spend time with my Tuscora family.

I sat next to Stacy on Aunt Sherry's old porch couch. She leaned close to my ear, so no one could hear. "What I tell you about your hair? That's your crown little girl. Take care of it." If it were one of my sister's the entire scenario would've been different. The whole street would've heard how nappy my hair was. Right along with a few more punchlines. Not thinking how their words would play a part in the way I viewed myself. I was a reminder of all the things they buried internally. I was a constant reminder of the parts they didn't like within themselves. The eyes are the windows to the soul. We all share the same eye expression. I call it the picket fence with nothing behind it expression. Myself, and all my siblings share it.

Stacy didn't waste anytime getting started on my hair. She made her friend get up, so she could fix my crown. While she's grooming my hair. My cousin shellie didn't waste any time before she started painting my nails. For that moment I felt like a child. Someone was finally responsible for me. I was relaxed.

I sat there for 2 1/2 hours as they talked to their friends about the neighborhood boys, neighborhood chicks they didn't like, and who they would beat up. There was no denying that both sides of my family were extremely tough. The difference between the two is the Greens will treat you like a bum in the street if you didn't fit in. The Morris side. My mom's side, when you're family that's it. They treat you as such. There aren't any feelings of inadequacy. Only loving reassurance. I appreciated that. It was something I felt only while in their presence. They love me. Never once failed at it. My mother had the most beautiful brother's, and sister's inside and out. Part Irish, Part Cherokee, and it showed! They would party and drink like grandpa Jack, and spiritually grounded and guided like grandma Lessie. We were a big rainbow coalition family. We loved each other in real life. It was fun listening to the gossip, but the were kids out. They were playing all sorts of games. From any bounce, kickball, and monkey in the middle. This was my chance to play, and be a kid once.

I must have jumped rope for hours, raced my cousins twenty-five times, and played the Junkyard Dog in a wrestling match. (Yes, I was a bit of a tomboy) I had a blast! That being said you know my heart broke when it was time to leave. We didn't visit often, so I didn't know how long before I could feel the love again. It's funny because before writing this book I couldn't reflect on those memories. Isn't it funny? The more you suppress, and block out pain: after while it becomes the only emotion that you feel. It's like when I would suppress one emotion I restricted myself from feeling the rest. I didn't figure this out until I was 42 years old and broken down to the floor. In a room full of total strangers.

I didn't say a word the whole ride home. I didn't want to leave. With those sad emotions I layed in the backseat until I fell asleep. It was a temporary fix for the mix of emotions running inside me. I barely knew how to process how I was feeling, so I went to sleep. Death had to be easy. Beginning at very young age life was hard for me.

Chapter Seven

Grown Before My Time

First day of high school, and I can't tell you how I made it. My guess school officials were tired of the wasted space. I could've stayed home because high school was like a daycare to me. A bunch of immature boys, and snootie, gossiping girls. I was holding down a household, reading and sorting bills, making dinner... Etc. I was too grown up for high school kids. I was doing for myself, and family what their parents were doing for them.

I was grown up. I knew how to be useful, as well as survive. I was going to be a good wife for somebody one day. I'm going to take care of my future husband. Keep myself a job, and be his financial partner. Make sure he's not too stressed about the bills. I'm going to have his babies. Love on them daily. Speak life, love, and prosperity to them. Pay attention, and help guide them. Most of all hear them, and address their needs. I wasn't going to be shit like my parents. My family was going to be perfect. Whatever it takes to keep my family happy, and my husband in love with me. The problem was finding a husband worthy. Especially in high school surrounded by boys. I was way too put together for their immature minds. Not knowing I should be enjoying life just as they were. Nope, at 15yrs old I wanted love, loyalty, commitment, protection, stability and structure. I want to be loved. Not even sure of who I am or my purpose in life. Clueless, I wanted someone to love me.

High school was not the place to find this. Hanging out with my cousin Nissa I would though. She knew all the hustlers, and I'd make a fine hustler's wife. One thing for sure, I knew how to keep my damn mouth closed. I'd leave school often, just to kick it with her. We'd leave Cleveland Heights and go to the east side of Cleveland known as "The Hough Heights." Now you'd think two little Heights girls had no business on Hough. Well, we weren't your average. We were tough. My cousin was 22, I was 15, but with hair and make up I could easily pass for twenty... So I did. Met myself a hustler by the name of C. Dubb. He was a smooth soft-spoken cat. Laid back, and had a strong presence. You'd never guess he was a killer. I was too shy to step to him, so I'd just stare. I watched him so hard I knew his every emotion. I even knew when he was lying. I was a people watcher. I knew expressions, body language, eyes, and demeanor. I knew when people were full of shit. Yet I would still second guess my instincts for some reason. I almost always would be right.

Nissa and I decided to go to the midnight league baseball game. We heard all the hoods most elite was going to be there. My only concern was with C. He had this strong presence. Kind of like my dad. He didn't say too much just like me. Never involved in any of the nonsense. He'd make his money and go. Outside of him being a hustler. C was pretty laid back. Plus he always dressed in black. Black as well as yellow are my two favorite colors. Black is a beautiful color, and yellow makes melanin radiant.

I was dressed in all white that day. I had on white Karl Kani jeans with a belly T-shirt, white Karl Kani jean jacket, and all white K-Swiss with the peanut butter sole. I had the sweetest T-boz cut, and you couldn't tell me a thing! I was no longer the little ugly duckling. I learned how to arch my eyebrows, and apply my makeup. Mattie started paying me to babysit, so getting "fresh" was nothing. People often told me I favored Toni Braxton. I didn't see that shit though.

Soon as we got to Thurgood Marshall I could smell the weed, and cigarettes in the air. You hear the cars roll up with their booming systems. Guys and girls drinking 40's in their best jewels and gear. Everybody trying to upstage the next. I didn't care about none of that shit. I wanted to be grown, but not stupid. I was stupid enough. I would never compete for fear of losing. I'll never get drunk, or do drugs because I've seen both change people I loved. One thing I knew for sure is I didn't want to be like the people I loved. So anything outside of a joint here and there wasn't my thing. I don't trust people, so I only smoked what I rolled. I knew a guy who was slipped a primo and he hasn't been the same since. His name was Curtis and he was my brother... A "sucka."

Nissa and I finally made it to our seats. We got a spot in the bleachers right behind C, and his crew. "Damn Lil Ma! You slid up in here looking like an angel in all that white." I was grinning from ear to ear! C, thought I was an angel. I quickly replied maybe I was meant to be your angel. He smiled, and said "all mine huh?" I smiled back and shyly nodded my head yes. With a sly grin he said. "We'll see Lil Ma." Then turned around to watch the game.

We're now in the 4th inning, and the crowd was kicking it! A few of the hustlers fired up a couple grills with hamburgers, hotdogs, and chicken. I had a joint in my Coach bag I rolled from earlier in the day. I saved it just for sitting on these uncomfortable bleachers. I've had my ass kicked in so much my bones would hurt from time to time. Sometimes swell, so I'd hit a joint a couple times then no more pain. The bleachers were taking a toll on my hips, and I didn't want to embarrass myself stumbling to get up. So, I sparked flame to what eased the physical pain.

Soon as I put fire to my joint C's brother Life comes fumbling out of nowhere towards us. He was a complete disarray. Not like he used to be. This was completely different. I knew what it was because I've seen this shit before. "What's good Lil bro?" Life was twenty five years old. Three years older than C. "You tell me big bro. What's up with that package I gave you?" C asked. Immediately Life started doing what I call the "shuck and jive" bullshit. The same shifty demeanor as my brother Curtis. "I got you baby bro. I been tied up with the baby moms." C laughed at the thought of his brother being whipped, but I knew better. He may have very well been whipped. But in that moment, his ass was getting high. Soon as he walked off to the hotdog stand I told C. You know you'll never see that package, or the money from it. I told him his brother was getting high. Why did I do that? His entire face changed. He looked at me as if I was a disgusting piece of shit. "Bitch how the fuck you know? You don't know me, or my brother to make assumptions like that." He frightened me with his anger. He was so pissed, he didn't even notice I opened my switchblade. I kept my hand on it in my pocket. If this frog leaped I was going to lung, and gut him like a fish. I'm not with being hit anymore. I simply replied no I don't know either of you. What I do know is people and their characteristics. Just as I came I left. My stupid big mouth got me in trouble again. I know what I felt in the presence of his brother. I knew hands down Life was hiding his new habit. I didn't mean to blurt it out the way I did. You know how the light bulb would pop up in cartoons when someone had an idea? That's kinda how it popped in my head. Then, the words came flying out my mouth sounding all "matter factly." I need some discretion with this big mouth of mine!

Chapter eight

The next day I didn't even bother with school. I caught the bus to Hough. I had a few nickel bags I needed to sell. My nephew was getting clowned at school. Mama bought him some Cleveland Browns tennis shoes from Payless Shoe Store. We all knew the Browns sucked! So did Payless shoes! I didn't know any that wanted, or wore their shoes. I promised I'd look out, and get him some sneakers. I was a full blown hustler now. At least so I thought. Hell, I most certainly advanced from babysitting for Mattie, cutting grass, carrying groceries, and washing dishes for the old ladies in the neighborhood. I was selling weed. I didn't want to do it. Hell, I wanted to be a nurse. School couldn't teach me, and my parents showed little to no interest. I had to survive before I was even old enough to work. I'm sure you asking by now why didn't this girl just speak up? I did. This one time my eighth grade year. Right before the school year ended.

It was my last year of junior high when I decided to speak up. I'm not sure why, or what made me finally talk. I do however remember nothing happening. I even had the bruises on my face when I decided to speak up, but somehow my clever parents wiggled their way out. It was somehow my clumsy behavior. Yeah... I walk around falling face first into shit. Go figure! I read the report written by the counselor sent to my home. She was even reluctant in her statement to believe my parents, but there was no further investigation. So, I said to hell with school, and everything it stands for. I need to eat, and I need shoes! The only thing I could depend on was my hustle, and myself.

Bagged up and ready to hustle I sold my first 20 bags with ease. I moved swiftly, didn't talk, and kept one hand on my knife. I was laid back, and the hustlers liked this. I wasn't loud, I didn't flag down cars, I didn't advertise strains. I simply would blow a joint with the biggest ballers in each crew. The leaders. I'd then politely let them know I had more if they needed anymore. My grass was different from what was going around Hough. I had this spoiled rich kid robbing his parents stash. They were two lesbian women that got high all day everyday. I couldn't understand why they smoked so much. It made them look, as well as be lazy. He hated their relationship. His mom left his crackhead dad for Lindsey the cosmetic plastic surgeon. I used his hatred for his two moms to my advantage. To fund my hustle. They kept large amounts of weed in garbage bags. He would give me a ziploc gallon freezer bag full once a week. All I had to do was get him those exclusive kicks a day before they came out. Nissa loud mouth was my connect for that. She worked at Foot Locker part time. I'd have her grab the kicks, plus some socks for gratitude. Toss her a bag for her efforts, and go make money. I had my routine on lock! I stayed under the radar. Didn't go out hustling everyday because I didn't want my face to be a regular. I knew if I got caught the police wouldn't care I was trying to survive, or want to hear my story. I'm just another animal that lacks self discipline to them. Its sad, but this is often how people like myself are looked at. People of color. That isn't my case. I simply fell through the cracks designed for me, and people that look like me. I paid so much attention to how the cops operated I forgot about the jackers, and robbers.

After spending three hours on the block I sold one hundred and thirteen bags. Some bagged as dimes, some bagged as nickels, but they all sold. I had more than enough to get my nephew some shoes, grab some groceries, and get a bus pass.

It's close to midnight, so I gotta clear out. Last bus leaves at 12:21. I stuffed my money in my pants, and got to stepping with my knife open. Hand in my pocket. I stayed ready for a frog to leap. I walked through the cut to get to the bus stop. It made me slightly sick to my stomach because the "bando's" (what we called the abandoned homes in the neighborhood) smelled like piss. I heard what sound like footsteps behind me. The moment I turned to see, I was bashed in the left side of my head with a powerful fist. Now clearly this is someone that didn't know me. If so they would've known I could take a blow just as well as give a mighty blow back. The moment I shook it off, and squared up with him. I saw the shock in his eyes. He knew whatever he was trying to pull wasn't going to be easy. "Chill lil mama. I don't wanna hurt yo pretty ass for real, but I need that cash up out you." I couldn't just turn it over. I had people depending on this money, hell depending on me! Just in that very moment I recognized the voice. Life...Is that you? Why did I say that! He charged at me like a raging bull. My body went flying to the ground, and my head hit a rock. Dazed, and too weak to fight him off he pulled all the money I had out my pants. Once he got the money he wasn't done. I knew what was next. In a weakened state I was fighting him for dear life. Please don't let this happen to me again. Another damn demon having its nasty way with me. I'm scrambling trying to feel for my knife, but it wasn't in my grasp. It must of flew out of my hand upon falling. I could feel the hope leave my body with every funky thrust he laid into my body. He was robbing me of all my hope and dignity... In a pile of piss filled leaves.

Shaking, and out of my mind from fear and adrenaline. I wouldn't give up. I was patting around on the ground trying to feel for my knife. At last! I found it! I jabbed that knife in the top of his shoulder so hard. It was like cutting cheese the way it pierced his flesh with ease. I then drug it as far down his back as I could before he hopped off. Soon as he got up I snatched off his ski mask. Sure as I thought it was Life punk ass! I blacked out from that moment.

The next thing I remember is walking on Crawford with one shoe on holding my pants together, shirt torn apart, and bleeding from my head. I walked past several people who were laughing. I heard a female voice say " somebody whooped her ass!" Then the laughter got louder. A male voice cosigned saying: "That, or somebody gave her some bad dope." I was far from ever being a damn crackhead! It was the crackhead that beat, robbed, and raped me! Suddenly I heard a familiar voice say I know her. Walking in a cloudy state I didn't even pay attention to him trying to catch up to me. By the time my eyes met with his, and I noticed it was C. I couldn't talk. I fell into his chest a screamed! I don't mean a loud cry either. I let out a sound of pain that made the whole block go quiet. Even the elders came outside. I was crying a puddle on this man's chest. C, then picked me up with tear filled eyes. As C carried me over to his car. He softly whispered in my ear. "Who did this to you? I will kill them." Remembering the last time I told him the truth he was pissed. I spoke the truth to my school officials before.

The school officials didn't believe me. They left me in the house of horrors. So, I lied. That was becoming normal for me. Lying, and hiding. I told him I didn't know. I did manage to tell him I sliced the person that assaulted me. I cut his ass real good, and deep down his back. He carefully placed me in the front seat of his car. C grabbed his gun from the glove compartment, and headed towards the short cut where I was raped. Twenty minutes went by, then I heard three gunshots. Pow! Pow! Pow! I remember the three shots sounding as if they said the words. YOU MUTHA FUCKA!! C finally emerged from the circle of piss filled abandoned homes. He passed his gun to Miss Minnie standing on the porch. She was the hood O.G. when she heard the shots it was clean up time. She knew what to do with a hot gun. He got in the car staring blankly straight ahead. "I should've believed you the first time Lil mama." From that day on I never mentioned Life's name again. C, and I were inseparable from that day forward. I never, ever spoke a word about what happened in the short cut between C, and his brother that night. I never spoke a word to anybody about what happened to me that night. I was hollow, numb, worn out, and grief stricken. I didn't do too much outside of my bedroom. I'd run my errands, but nothing else. I simply didn't want to be bothered. At this point I was exhausted with people. I wanted nothing more than to be in my bedroom. Drowning out my life with my headphones on. I often stayed in bed watching tv. I was in love with my personal space, and solitude. I didn't have to deal with anyone, and no one could hurt me. To this very day I have to have my periods of solitude. Especially when I'm going through something heavy. I don't think anyone took notice, or deemed this behavior as odd. I sure as hell wasn't. It was my comfort zone. I had no clue this was an ongoing cycle. A cycle of what I now know to be depression, and P.T.S.D.

Chapter Nine

C, And CiCi

It's been about two weeks since I last hung out on Hough. At home bored out of my mind the phone rings. It's Nissa calling. Finally! I got some action! Her daughter's father was having a huge birthday bash, and I should come out with my "crybaby ass". She yelled through the phone. Obviously she was already pumped up to go. I was extremely reluctant at first. I wasn't sure I'd be safe. Especially the embarrassment I'd encountered when I told C the truth about his brother Life. I was also on the other hand bored out of my mind with a house full of angry people. Screw it! I'm going to the party! I mean anything is better than being in this damn place. The demon moved back in the house, and I would often feel uneasy at home. I tried my best to not be around when I knew the demon was at home. I wasn't the same as I used to be. This person wasn't taking it anymore. I've finally reached my breaking point. I couldn't handle being violated in that way by anyone again. The thought of it would terrify the shit out of me. I began to tremble while holding the phone. I got so caught up in my thoughts. I'd completely forgotten that Nissa was on the phone. "Bitch here you go zoning out. You going or not?" I quickly said yes, and ended the call. The simple thought would take me back to the very moment I was violated. I didn't want to open that door. I was getting ready for a party. That negative energy would later leave me feeling empty, and out of place. Feelings I didn't need while trying my best to fit in. While taking a long hot shower I cried my eyes out. It was my temporary release. I simply wanted to be free from haunting hardships. I wanted to be a teenager. I wanted life like my peers without having to take care of everyone, and everything for once. I got dress, and headed out making sure to slam the door behind me. I hate living in this house I said to myself walking down the street. At least the demon on Hough no longer exists... So I thought.

We got to the party, and the Dj was playing my song. Jackin For Beats by Ice Cube. I walked through the door "two steppin." I was instantly drawn to the beat. Music made me happy, and I loved to dance. I was about to bust out doing "the wop" (one of my favorite dances to do.) When Nissa pointed gesturing for me to look over my shoulder. So much for distracting my thoughts. The moment I turned around. I saw C dressed in all black. Black Guess Jeans, Guess sweatshirt, red Fila tennis shoes, with a red Chicago Bulls pro model cap. He was looking damn good! They way he yelled my name immediately brought me back to reality. By the sound of his voice something needed my attention. His voice barrelled over the speakers like a got damn bullhorn! When C called my name it seemed like everyone in the party started looking at me. You would've thought C was my father the way he yelled my name across a room full of people. He obviously wanted to talk to me about something, so I walked over to him.. "What's up CiCi? Let me holla at you for a minute." He asked with a puzzled expression. Reluctantly, I agreed to follow C outside. But, not before opening my pocket blade. This conversation will determine if my knife will leave my pocket. It's been a little over two weeks since I last saw C. I told this man his brother was a crack addict, and a rapist. Not to mention, I'm almost certain C murdered him. I haven't seen any sign of his brother since that day. Hell, I was confined to my room waiting out the intense sadness that plagued my life. He could very well be alive and well. Somewhere waiting for C to take me out. All these thoughts raced through my mind. For now I knew better. He wasn't about to walk me outside to meet my demise that easy. Not without a fight, or getting his ass cut. I didn't trust men, and never met a human I feared.

We made it through the wall to wall party, finally making outside. C, and I walked over to a quiet spot out in the open. We were in a field next door to the house party. The field was well lit from the street lights. So, hopefully there's no shady business going on. We both took a seat on a couple of milk crates, found stacked near the side of the house. C, pulled a blunt from his ear. He lit it, and handed it to me. He noticed I was reluctant to take it. I told him that I was ok. Smoking already rolled up weed wasn't my thing. No offense to you, but I don't know you to know your habits. I told C. Making sure to speak my words slow, and easy. The last thing I needed was for him to take offense to what I said. "I like that about you Lil mama. You not pressed for somebody else's shit. Not like the rest of these blunt berry hoes. Tell me something. How did you know my brother was smoking crack?" I was completely caught off guard! I wasn't ready for that question. I knew if I told him the truth he'd think I'm crazy. I wasn't that quick on my toes, so for the first time without being afraid. I told him the truth.

I peeped his "steelo." His movements, body language, and eye contact. Those were all dead ringers for me. I calmly told C. I wanted to keep a low tone while speaking. Giving him a clue that the questions were making me uncomfortable. Hopefully this will keep him from asking any questions about the encounter I had with his brother. That was something I didn't want to talk about. Not ever! I couldn't bring myself to talk about it. Once I'd let my mind go back to a traumatic experience it would overwhelmed my present mood. I'm mentally right back in that helpless position. I can feel, and even smell everything from that day. I sat there rocking back, and forth in my seat. I almost wet myself afraid of the thought C may ask about it. I to this very day have trouble reliving past traumas. Hell, I'm pissing like a racehorse if I'm in a room full of unfamiliar men. So, I didn't want this man to ask me questions that'll send me back reliving traumas.

C looked at me with a peculiar grin. "I need you on my team. I need my lady to peep game when I'm slipping." Relieved by his response. I eagerly replied. I need to be your lady! I mean why not? He has already shown that he'll protect me. We always seem to enjoy each other's company. So on that day I became C"s lady. From that day forward it was C, and CiCi. We were inseparable.

I was spending little to no time at home now. The demon moved back into the house of horrors, and I had to get my butt out of there. I remember calling C in the middle of his nightly count. Something he did every night at about 3am. It was his last round to collect his money from the street. I was screaming, and crying by the time he answered. I was telling him how I was tired of the demon! He'd moved back in, and I was a grown woman now! I wasn't having it! When I was a child I couldn't protect myself. I would fight as hard as I could with it! I wasn't strong enough to stop him from doing his deed. I thought I would be able to stop him as a young adult. I was wrong. I knew if I didn't get out of there I was going to kill this nasty mutha fucka.

Soon as I hung up the phone I started packing up my belongings. By the time I got finished, C was already outside. Sitting in his all black Cadillac Eldorado. His windows were tinted so he couldn't notice my disheveled expression. Once I got inside he knew something was up. I most definitely wasn't behaving like myself. I had the same look in my eyes when his brother had his way with me. I felt tarnished, nasty, embarrassed, violated, most of all lost. Lost, and dirty!

He didn't say a word the entire drive. We went back to his place. He carried me through the doors, and placed me gently on the couch. After spending about ten minutes in the bathroom. C lifted my limp body, slowly removing my clothing. He carried my now naked body to a hot bubble bath that he'd prepared just for me. As he washed me from head to toe he gently planted soft kisses on my neck, and forehead. Once C was done giving me a bath, and moisturizing my body. I was carried to his bedroom, and placed in his California king bed. The entire bed was laced with red satin sheets, pillows, and comforter. He climbed in behind me. C took me in his arms, and held me tightly. His grasp Reassuring me that I was safe with him. I remember feeling at ease. At that moment I did feel safe in C's arms. That night I made love to a man willingly. For the first time in my life I wanted to have sex, and it was beautiful. I watched him while he slept. Looking at him thinking to myself. Is this the man who will finally love, and protect me? Will I be safe with this man? I fell asleep with ease. I was safe, and free from worry.

The next morning was more delightful. Not to mention the fridge, and cupboards were filled with food. I was so grateful for the way he made me feel. I planned to make him a breakfast fit for a king. After a long hot shower I proceeded straight to the kitchen. I was going to to make C, and I breakfast. Bacon, sausage, eggs, grits, and toast. I ironed his clothes, then I prepared his plate. I greeted my man at the table with a smile. I was wearing a sheer red sexy pajama set. I wanted to be his entire package. "Damn baby you the best." His statement made me smile. He took his seat at the head of the table. I had his napkin folded like a crown on his plate. It was time for my king to eat. Just as I was about to take a seat someone started bamming on the door. I didn't move. I watched C wipe his mouth, and head to the door. It was Mick on the other side of the door. He was C's right hand man. C opened the door just to hear Mick say it's been handled. He closed the door then sat down with me to finish his breakfast. We laughed, and ate together for about an hour. He talked about my snoring, and I denied it ever happened. When we finished breakfast. C, gave me a fist full of cash. He told me to go shopping for groceries and clothes. "You'll be safe. You don't have to worry about Life, or anyone anymore. You're my girl now. Nobody will dare step to you. I'm Sure you know Life isn't coming back, so you have no worries." I didn't know what to say, or think about what C was saying to me. I didn't want to think about him killing his brother. I for damn sure didn't want to be reminded of my trauma with his brother. So, I counted out three thousand dollars as if he wasn't talking. I got up, and got myself ready to go shopping. I felt absolutely nothing for what he just said. Fuck it! I went shopping, and back with no problems.

Two months into our relationship, and I was CiCi The Homemaker. I fell head first into wife mode. Doing so came with ease. I felt protected with C, so therefore I was eager to please him. I wanted him to know I appreciate him. One thing I knew above all else was how to serve, and please people. The only time I mattered is when I took care of people. It was also something that I was good at doing. I wanted to make a difference, and matter to C. I didn't mean anything to anyone else. I wanted to mean something to the man that made me feel safe.

I must've bought food from three different grocery stores today. I shut the mall down, and even had time to have lunch with a homeless gay guy named Damon. He would always sleep on the vent outside of Subway sandwich shop downtown on twelfth street. This man had an amazing voice! Every time I would go downtown I'd make it my business to show him love, and give nourishment when I was able to do so. He was a good soul that simply lost his way. He was also super smart. We'd sit and talk for hours about any and every thing. We'd talk about time, space, people, Africa, food. You name it we've discussed it. Right in the middle of lunch I got seriously ill. I almost didn't make it to the bathroom before vomiting up my entire lunch. I didn't even close the bathroom stall. It was like a volcano erupted. As I cleaned myself up in the sink. There was an older African American woman next to me in the mirror. She was applying wet & wild Ruby red lipstick. She looked at me and said "You're pregnant!" I thought to myself what does she know. She had more lipstick on her teeth than lips. I'm going to need her to figure her life out before telling me about mine. I smiled at the old woman dressed in yellow, and made my exit out of the bathroom.

When I returned to the booth Damon, and I shared. I immediately apologized. Our conversation was just beginning to gain depth. I hated having to cut our conversation short, but I was extremely sick to my stomach. I gathered my things, and started heading towards the door. He stopped me in mid stride. Damon was a funny man, so he apologized if his oder made me sick. I reassured him his presence was more powerful than his smell. I asked him to forgive me, but I had to go.

I was now nauseous and tired. I dropped the groceries off at C's then went to the house of horrors to get more clothes. There was no sign of the Demon so, I decided to take a nap. My stomach was still feeling a bit queasy. My body felt worn out from simply shopping. I was extremely exhausted for some reason.

About an hour, or so into my nap. I was awakened by my dad cursing mama out again. He was hungry and there wasn't much to cook in the house. He was telling my mother once again, she wasn't worth a shit. This wasn't anything new to me. I'm not sure if the words bothered mama much anymore. I knew it made me feel sad to hear him speak to her like trash. I texted C to come get me. There was no reason for me to hear the B.S. I grabbed my belongings, and got up to leave the house of horrors for good. Soon as I got to the steps, pops stopped me in my tracks. "Where the hell do you think you're going? That school called here talking about you stopped coming." I was completely caught off guard because for the last year I've been coming and going as I pleased and no one noticed. I was the invisible woman until someone needed something, or I did something wrong. When I finally did answer. I said what came to mind. I'm going to get something to eat with C. That was the first thing came to my head. I was a little hungry, so I went with it. Why daddy? Do you need something? I was so eager to be useful. "Yeah I'm hungry. Bring me and your mama a polish boy back." I said okay, then I flew past him so fast. I hated that house. It was too much! Here

I am 15 years old, and I am responsible for feeding my parents. When the truth is that someone needed to be responsible for me. I was still a child. I hopped in the car with C, and we rolled out. I wasn't ever going back to that house, so I stayed the night with my man. I fell asleep in his arms thinking to myself how perfect he would be if he wasn't a drug dealer. I mean the stuff he sold ruined people. Including my brother. I put it to the back of my mind. At least it wasn't my parents house. Even though C was a drug dealer. I felt safe here. At this time I wasn't being abused, or maybe I hadn't taken notice.

I woke up the next morning sick as ever! I hurled everywhere! C seemed to be happy about this. What are you so happy about? I asked him. "The mother of my child." He replied, with a sly smirk on his face. I wasn't smiling though. I was instantly terrified at the thought. I can't be pregnant. I was only fifteen years old lying to this man saying that I was twenty years old. C, was technically my first, but the truth is the demon ruined that, and me. I felt filthy, and uncomfortable in my own skin. Just thinking about it made me hurl again. C wasn't wasting any time. Soon as I opened the bathroom door there he was. Standing there with a pregnancy test in his hand. I gotta admit his eagerness, and excitement was adorable. So, I went ahead to the bathroom. My heart started beating faster as I peed on the stick. Well I'll be damned! Two lines formed almost instantly! It was official... I was pregnant.

I'm not sure if I expressed any emotion at all. C jumped for joy! He got on the phone, and started ordering cigars. He looked me in the eyes and told me that I was never going home. He said he didn't know what happened to me in that house, and he didn't want to know. He knew I went in one way, and I'd come out depressed. He was taking me to get all of my things, and I was beyond excited. I would grab a few things here and there. I never took everything I owned. I didn't want C to think I was getting too comfortable. Truth is I was too comfortable for my own good.

I hurriedly ran through the house of horrors door, and up the stairs. I was leaving this place, and never coming back. When I got to the top of the stairs. My father was there waiting to greet me. "What happened to me and your mama food?" Oh shit! I forgot all about I had to feed them. I ended up getting distracted with the pregnancy test it slipped my mind. I was shaking in my boots! Not for long though. Pops punched me so hard he sent me flying backwards down the stairs. I hit the wall on the second landing, and before I could get up to run he punched me again in the temple. Before passing out, I saw my mother sitting in her rocking chair. I remember asking her to help me. She didn't even look at me. As I saw tears falling from her eyes I felt so bad for her. She had to watch him beat the hell out of me.

I took the beating, and prayed that my baby wasn't hurt. I was completely taken back with emotions. I wasn't even a woman at this moment. I felt like I was less than nothing at this point... Absolutely nothing.

By the time I went back to the car I was beat in one inch of my life. I even wet my clothes, and I was embarrassed for C to see me. My entire being was mentally done. When I got in the car, C was livid at the sight of me. "What the fuck happened in there? Don't nobody disrespect me, and what's mine! Nobody! You not his no more. You mine!" C, said as two veins popped out of his forehead. He punched the dash with each word he said. I knew he was furious! That very moment is when I thought possession was love, and protection. I convinced C I was good, let's go home. I had enough excitement for one day.

Chapter Ten

When we arrived home C couldn't wait to grill me. He was silent the whole drive home, so i knew he wanted answers. "What the fuck is up CiCi? I don't want to hear no bullshit story. How do you think this shit make me look? People can do what they want to C's girl? I have to walk around with you looking like that. The least you can do is tell me who did it. I asked C if I could please have a moment to get myself together, and clean up. I was soiled with urine, and my body was sore from the beating I just took. I had no clue how I was going to explain this. What I was really trying to do is buy some time. I didn't know how to explain what happened. Not to mention he had another thing coming if he thought I would let him hurt my father. I stayed in that shower for almost an hour. I had no idea what I was going to say to this obviously angry man.

I sat down next to C as if nothing happened. What are you watching? He didn't find my behavior amusing. "Don't fucking play with me CiCi. What the fuck happened to your face?" I couldn't stall him any longer, so I told him the truth. I got into a disagreement with my father. I said it firm, and clear. Loud enough for C to hear the conviction in my voice. He needed to know I wasn't playing. It's between my father, and I. I replied to C. That's none of your concern what we go through. It's our business. Be grateful it has nothing to do with you. C looked at me as if he wanted to punch me in the face. I didn't want to prove myself right, so I stopped talking. "I'm going to leave the shit alone. I'm sure your little slick ass mouth is what got you fucked up. Make that your last time speaking to me like you're crazy." I knew then my intuition wasn't failing me. I told him the day he hit me he better be ready to fight. He looked me in the eye with a straight face. Then he proceeded to say. "There won't be a fight. I will knock you the fuck out. Put your ass to sleep, and make you think about it." I saw jail flash before my eyes. I thought to myself. I don't want to kill this man. I smiled, and watched tv. C went where ever to do whatever it is he does I didn't care. Just as long as he didn't put his hands on me.

I woke up the next morning starving. This pregnancy had me eating sun up to sun down. I loved cereal, so I had two bowls every morning. Captain Crunch Berries, and Fruity Pebbles. Not sure if I have a baby bump, or pudgy from inhaling food all day. C didn't come home, and to tell the truth I wasn't upset at all. I was in one of my solitude phases. My most favorite of all. I truly enjoyed being alone. When you have a huge family. You see different people, and their many phases. You share life experiences, as well as emotional highs, and lows. So it's like you've seen everything, so you feel everything. That's why I would often feel drained after spending the holidays with family and friends. I would show up for a function have a blast, love you to death, and I won't talk to you again for a month or two. No phone calls, text, not even a bat signal. I need that solitude to process, and clear out all the different emotions encountered. Some friends, and family would swear I was funny acting. Others, a mere two or three understood. That's simply CiCi. And, CiCi had to recharge.

Chapter Eleven

History Repeats Itself

I'm big as a house and literally barefoot and pregnant. My nose was huge, neck turned black and I didn't have the energy for anything anymore. This pregnancy was taking its toll on me for sure. So was my relationship with C. I wasn't allowed to leave unless he knew where I was going and who I was going with. I was no longer allowed to hang at The rec center because it was too many guys there. I couldn't even go to the park anymore. He knew how I loved sitting in nature with a pen and a pad. He didn't hesitate to take that from me as well. He said no lady of his is gonna be on some Mary Poppins, Jill Scott, bullshit. I wanted him to love me, so I was willing to give up all of me to feel the one thing I longed for. I was truly fooling myself. I didn't even know myself, or love myself. How could I expect him to love me?

My entire pregnancy I felt miserable. I was no longer his angel. I was the clingy little trophy he'd take off the shelf when he felt like it. I would hear rumors of him around town with other women. Hell, some nights he wouldn't come home. Still, to me this was better than being at the house where I grew up...I guess. Before I knew it I was behaving just like my mother. C had been gone for two days, and he finally decided to come home. He didn't even say hello. He came through the door, tossed his keys on the counter, then started making demands. "Make me something to eat I'm starving." He said in the most demanding voice. The tone I often heard him use, when checking people about his money. I didn't want to fall out with him. He'd just came home, and I didn't want him to leave again. So, I got up, and did as I was told. If I make him a feast, he'll stay home with me. I thought to myself. Soon as we sat down to eat. I made the mistake of asking C where he'd been. He looked me in the eye with a hard cold stare. "You don't make shit to ask me shit. Stay in your place CiCi." I shut up quick. Again, thinking to myself I didn't want him to leave. I didn't ask another question about his whereabouts. I finished my food quietly in tears. As I got up to wash the dishes. I could feel my sonshine moving. My due date was getting really close. With each day passing, C was getting more, and more possessive. He was hardly around, and I wasn't allowed to leave the house. I remember thinking to myself what happened to the protective gentleman I met? Was this him the whole time? How did I get in this situation?

A week had gone by, and I haven't heard from C. He wouldn't answer my calls or pages. I remember thinking to myself what if I was in labor? Will he be this way when the sun is born? I had a flash of my mother, and father. Then I looked at myself. I need a plan and quick! I'll be damn my child whom I have yet to meet feel anything like I did growing up. My sun will never question my love for him. His light shines so bright within my dark world it's my duty to fill his with love, and protection. I rubbed my belly and promised that nothing will come before my sonshine.

I woke up the next day, and headed for the shoebox. Since about 11 weeks into my pregnancy, I began keeping a stash of money in a shoebox. I kept it buried wrapped in plastic near my little garden in the backyard. Winter months I'd transfer them to a loose floorboard in the house. Every penny C threw at me, down to every penny I skimmed off the top was in this box. This box was my way out. In six to seven months I had a little over twenty two thousand dollars. I added another thousand to it, and headed back inside. Soon as my feet hit the kitchen floor my water broke. It was time to meet my sonshine!

I was in so much pain in the back of that two door Buick Regal. My father was driving like a bat out of hell, and mama just holding on to me while I cussed better than Richard Pryor. I had to call my parents for a ride to the hospital. I didn't want to be alone,and or with one of C's goons. C, was out on another one of his rendezvous, and he was anywhere to be found. Pop's was still my pops no matter what. He made sure to remind me that having a baby didn't make me grown. That he would knock my head off at any given moment for cussing. I didn't care though. I was in the worst pain of my life!

After spending twenty-three hours in the labor, and delivery unit. I finally met my baby boy. I was holding the most beautiful baby boy in the world. He was in my arms, and he was mine. Born weighing 7 lbs 6 ounces, he was still, so tiny and fragile to me. I remember holding him just staring at him for hours. At that very moment I dedicated my life to making him an awesome boy. As well as an even greater man. He will be nothing like the men in my life. I will make sure of that. My son will be great! Carter Joseph Rosetti Jr. My sonshine!

Lil Carter is now a year old, and beginning to walk. That one shoe box I had has now grown into three boxes. It was my seventeenth birthday, and Big Carter was throwing this huge party for me. The house was all decked out in decorations. The yard was set up for a luau. I wasn't very excited about having a party. It felt more like C's party than mine. The entire party was filled with only his guest, and family. He owned me, so he chose who I shared my time with. I spent most of the party playing in the grass with Baby Carter. I refused to call him Lil C like everyone else. He was mine too. I knew who the man C really was. I knew what he represented. My child is so much more than that. I refused to affiliate his character with the character of his father.

I noticed Carter getting the sleepy face, and I was exhausted from entertaining a bunch of people I didn't care about. So, there was little to no regrets cutting out early. I gathered our things, grabbed Carter, and headed in the house. Just before I got to the patio stairs, C stopped me in my tracks. He was drunk, and wobbly when he approached me. Slurring the words. "Where you going?" I was extremely exhausted, and I didn't want to fight with him. I'm going Inside C. Lil Carter is most definitely ready for a nap, and I've had enough of this party. The party that you clearly threw for yourself! I knew better than to talk to C like that. I was extremely tired, and he was frustrating me with his possessive behavior. The moment I turned around to walk in the house he hit me. C, hit me so hard I saw a flash of lights. Followed by his voice screaming the words "you ungrateful bitch!" He hit me so hard in the back of the head he literally knocked my lights out. When I finally woke up still on the kitchen floor where he laid me out. The party was cleared out, and I saw Baby Carter sitting on the floor next to me. He diaper was soaked, and he was screaming at the top of his lungs. I grabbed my baby cleaned him and myself up. I headed to my room. I located the loose floorboard where I keep my shoe boxes. I'd stashed more than enough money. It was now time to get myself, and my baby the hell out of there! I threw some clothes for Lil Carter, and I in garbage bags, then called a cab. I had to protect my sonshine. The only problem, I had nowhere to go. The house of horrors was worse than being with C. Too many people living there would have too much influence on my son. That day we moved into the Charterhouse hotel. The very next day I started looking for apartments. I was an emotional wreck at this point in my life.

My mental state had fallen apart. All I knew was how to keep going, and how to survive, show no fear, and handle your business. I held it together because only the weak fall apart, or beg. In my tribe we do what we gotta do. Not knowing behaving this way only made me more invisible. Invisible to myself and the people around me. I had no clue who I was. I looked to others to fulfil me, and tied my worth to how others saw me. At that moment I was looking bad, so I felt worthless, and foolish.

I found an apartment, but age was an issue. I said screw it! Changed my birth year... Boom! I'm 18. Carter, and I were the new proud renters of a two bedroom apartment. I slowly, but surely started fixing up the place. I'm great with building, decoration, all sorts of crafts. Fixing up our new home came easy. The cost was little to nothing because most of the materials were second hand. I enjoyed making, and building things as much as I enjoyed writing. I was slowly but surely making a home for Carter, and I.

After fixing up the place, I finally decided to have some family over. When it became close to time for the guests to arrive. I began to get restless. It's been close to three years now since I ran away from C. I was not only restless. I was lonely. My homegirl Nissa arrived first. She didn't waste any time with her interrogation. "Bitch when's the last time you had a man in ya life?" I don't need one. I replied swiftly. Hoping to shut down her line of questioning. "Don't need one? Or don't know how to pick one?" Nissa was my best friend because she kept it real. She also got on my nerves because she kept it too real. I yelled, Girl both! We bust out laughing. No one else showed up to my dinner party, so Nissa and I had a feast. We drank two bottles of wine, laughed, danced, cried, then passed out.

The next morning I woke up to Nissa knocked out on the couch, and someone at my door knocking like the police. I knew she was staying the night once we finished a pint of Hennessey after drinking two bottles of wine. I flung open the door to see a handsome Puerto Rican man about 5'5 standing there. A little short for my taste. Still, he was quite handsome. Can I help you? I asked all funky like. I had to do something to break my awkward gaze. "I'm sorry to bother you miss, does a man by the name of Mike live here? I've been away for a couple of years, and this was the last address I had for my homie." No one lives here by that name. You must have been gone for a long period of time. You have clearly lost track of time. He looked at me Baffled, so he didn't have to ask me to elaborate. I told him I'd been living here for three years. Maybe this Mike, or yourself has been a little longer than you thought. "You funny." He replied. "You're absolutely right. I visit my people upstairs, and I peeped you out. I like how you move. You're real low key." "She ain't got no man!" Nissa rude ass screamed from the couch in the middle of the poor man's sentence. Please excuse her, I asked. The poor thing has tourettes. I said jokingly. Look... I'm flattered you find me minding my business attractive. Mr? "Jerry, just call me Jerry." Well, Mr. Jerry it just so happens I am dating someone. Neither him, or I take too kindly to strange men knocking on my door. Make this your first, and last time. Soon as I slammed the door. I heard the poor man saying I'm sorry through the wood. I told Nissa to mind her damn business. She replied I am her business. Laughing to myself I couldn't argue with the woman. Besides, it was Carter, and workout time. I got his stroller, loaded in the usual. Snacks, toys, for Carter, couple free weights, blanket, and water. I'd power walk through the park while Carter chilled in the stroller checking out the scenery. Then spread out my blanket. This means snack time for Carter, squats, weights, and lunges for me. We made a great team together Carter, and I. On the power walk back I noticed edible arrangements, and flowerama delivery trucks in front of my building. When I got a little closer I noticed they were at my door! Two dozen red roses, 24 chocolate covered strawberries. All for a simple girl who hates roses. My mom planted rose bushes all around my childhood home. I can't tell you why I'm not the flowers and candy kinda girl. I knew those roses my mom planted surrounded a house full of shit. Time spent is far more precious than money to me. It took all of 10mins to make the calls for a delivery. Now, making something for me... That takes time, creativity, and work. The simplest things can be major for me. I love art. I am art. "Ya" feel me?

I tossed the roses on the counter, and smashed a couple berries with Carter. It was now bath time for Carter, and shower time for me. It was a lazy Saturday afternoon for my sonshine, and I. After dinner, and watching a couple of Carter's animated tv shows. I noticed his eyes were getting heavy. Carter was out like a light by 8:55pm. I poured myself a glass of chardonnay, and headed to my backyard porch to relax. I made a small pit, and patio furniture I made myself, from pallets I collected from the local grocery stores. I had a nice feng shui going on. Kinda like, IKEA meets pier one type of scenery. Perfect for the simple earthy chick that loved sunflowers, such as myself. The wine, fire pit, and long comfy sundress had me feeling all Sex In The "Cityish". I was straight chillin. That's until the little guy Jerry walked out of the back door of my building. He headed straight for my direction. "See you're so chill. I first peeped ya porch. I thought it was a dopest chill spot ever. Then my people told me they watched you build it. I couldn't believe it at first. I had to get a look at the chick that'll build her own porch furniture out of pallets. That actually looks dope as fuck! Then one early ass morning I caught a glimpse of you. I think you were meditating. You looked so beautiful to me CiCi. The sun was just beginning to rise, and the way the sunlight hit body. It made your skin glow! it shining just like brass. Then you opened your eyes, and killed the game. It's like the sun illuminate the gold flakes in your light brown eyes... Simply beautiful. I would've never guessed you were a mean lady that would slam a door in someone's face." I could not lie to myself. The short stack of flapjacks was super hot. No one ever noticed me in the way he did. I was flattered, and literally speechless. I would have never guessed that he was Latino. Not without the kiss me I'm Boricua t-shirt he wore during our first encounter. He looked more of an Italian lineage to me. Light with super dark hair. Like a greaser from the Outsiders type of look. The kinda guy that can make a simple pair of jeans, and t-shirt look dope. Something like myself. Art.. You feel me? I was nobody's "sucka", so I couldn't tell this short ass man his words were melting this chocolate from the inside out. So, I told him that I was on point with my first thoughts of him. I told him that I guessed he was a stalker when he first knocked on my door. We both bust out laughing.

Would you like to join me on the porch for a glass of wine? I barely got the words out of my mouth before he was climbing the porch. Forget about taking the stairs, and using the door. He seemed eager to join me. That made me smile. I grabbed the bottle from the counter, and another glass. I then joined him by the fire pit. "You made all of this by yourself?" Yes. I get a little antsy sometimes, and building things kinda slow things down for me a bit. If that makes any sense to you? He replied. "It makes perfect sense." He wanted in, so if I said pigs could fly it would make perfect sense to the guy trying to get laid. He wasn't about to get me wide open looking for his short ass in daylight with a flashlight. Then he elaborated, "you're keeping your hands as well as your mind busy. You get to focus on one thing, and it chills the overload of thoughts that makes you antsy. You sooth the busy body in you. While at the same time you're moving, and being productive. I get it." Little man had me blushing, feeling all giddy inside. He finished off the bottle of wine by himself. I was good after my second glass. I don't like drinking too much. I hate the sick queasy feeling that comes with it. One of the ugliest things to see is a woman sloppy drunk off her ass. It simply wasn't my thing. I guess he was pretty buzzed because his next question almost threw me out of my chair. "Why are you so stiff faced? Don't get me wrong you're absolutely beautiful. Your face sometimes lack expression or emotion. Like tonight when you smile you que yourself to do so. Behind the smile are those beautiful sad, lost eyes. I get chills when I get caught up in your gaze." I was at an absolute loss for words. I couldn't respond. I was lost, and in pain. How could he see through my mask? The one I thought I wore so well. He even explained my antsy behavior better than I ever could. After that I no longer wanted his company around. He saw too much of me. I was too ashamed to let myself be vulnerable, so I never spoke to him again. After a month of me avoiding him, and being rude. He finally backed off. It was a very long time before I would let anyone in my life intimately again.

Chapter twelve

By the time I turned 27 I was a functioning mess. I never took the time to fully address the traumas I'd encountered throughout my life. I was an absolute nervous wreck!

I'm not sure if I even took the time to mourn the loss of my mother. My mother suffered a massive stroke around my seventeenth birthday. The damage from it left her unresponsive. She remained unresponsive for ten years, before her soul transcended. I remember feeling like my life didn't have meaning. I felt empty, and unfulfilled.

I need a job! That's something I would never be without. I loved being able to take care of myself. I also had Carter to support. Who knew that my need for a job, would introduce me to my second son's father. The man, I literally almost allowed to destroy me.

Nissa had a job, working for a small family owned restaurant. Nissa worked two different positions. She'd work during the day as a part time food prep. Then Nissa, would return in the evening, and work as a line cook.

I ended up getting a job in the restaurant through Nissa. I worked full time, as a hostess. The restaurant was located in the downtown Cleveland area, and the food was awesome. Phil's Place was the only restaurant in downtown Cleveland serving soul food. Not to mention the Upscale atmosphere. The restaurant was small, but made for an intimate dining experience.

I'd just punched in for the day, when I noticed an unfamiliar face walk by. I didn't want to be bothered with small talk, so I didn't pay the new guy any attention. I'd just started to accept my mother's death. I didn't handling my mother's death too well, so I wasn't engaging in small talk. I wanted to do my job and go home.

I was minding my own business at work today. We'd just cleared out the lunch rush, when I finally decided to take a seat. That's when Nissa walked to my station. She looked as if she was marching towards me. Nissa's eyes were wide open, and she was smiling from ear to ear.

She started going on, and on about this new guy hired during my leave. After about five minutes of of her rambling, I asked who the guy was. Finally, she told me his name was, Shelton.

Shelton, began working at the restaurant as a server, but also trained as a cook. Nissa couldn't wait to mention how "he was nice looking, and that I should check him out." I told Nissa I wasn't in the mood to meet anyone, and continued to wipe down menus.

She laughed, while brushing me off. "Too late! He's heading this way right now.

I looked up only to see this slim, peanut head, funny looking dude walking towards us. I couldn't help giving Nissa the "I should punch you in the face look".

"What bitch?" She asked, while twisting her lips at me.

I told her that tdude resembled, a small head E.T. "phone home."

We both began to laugh our ass off. That's when Shelton finally approached us at the hostess stand.

"What's so funny ladies?" Nissa was extremely rude. She looked the peanut head bandit in the eyes, and said... "You!" Nissa, and I shared another laugh at Shelton's expense.

He quickly brushed it off, and asked Nissa if "I was the home girl she'd been telling him about. Nissa replied in her most ghetto fabulous tone. "Yes! That's my dawg!"

He smiled at me, then said I reminded him of his sister.

Me being a smart ass. I told him that his sister must be a very beautiful woman. He began to smile again, and agreed. Although, he was kinda funny looking. He had a beautiful smile. His smile made his eyes appear to be innocent. He had the coolest personality, and seemed to be a humble soul.

It wasn't long before we started hanging out together. We'd meet up after work for drinks, movies, bowling, dinner. Whatever we wanted to do in each other's company. Afterwards, I'd give him a lift home. We didn't live far from each other. The drive was merely ten minutes tops. So,

I didn't mind giving him a lift. Besides, he was good company. He kept me laughing, and my mind off my troubled past. As time went on Shelton, and I grew closer. After eight months of seeing each other almost everyday. That's when

Shelton asked the question that changed my life forever.

Shelton, and I both worked a double shift. We were exhausted, and ready for bed. We've been dating for quite some time now, and I would spend most of my time at his place.

We walked in the door, heading straight towards the shower. Not wasting any time, we both stripped down to our birthday suits. Shelton turned on the shower, then kissed me softly on the lips. I followed him in the shower, where we kissed again. That's when he said it. The words that changed my life. " I love you CiCi. I've never met anyone like you. You're cool as hell, you always have your own money, you don't mind paying the bill, and you don't touch my remote." We both laughed, then Shelton kissed me softly before finishing up with our shower.

Once dried off, It was time to moisturize, and slip on one of Shelton's t-shirts. Shelton, literally hopped in bed wearing only his boxers. He had this devilish grin on his face. I knew he was up to something in that head of his. Before I could ask Shelton cut me off. "CiCi you want to move in? I mean we're practically living together anyway." He did have a point. A two income household does sound really nice. Why not! Less than three months later. Shelton,and I began sharing the address.

He treated Carter and I like we were his family. He had a beautiful daughter of his own. She was only two years old, and her name was Savannah. She was absolutely adorable! Very polite, quiet, with a big personality! I enjoyed when he'd bring her over. He didn't talk much about her mom, but I knew she hated his guts. I didn't get involved. Helped out where I could, and left the affairs of their daughter up to them. I did however enjoy spending time with her.

The first year living together things were great! We were dating for a year and three months when things began to change. The restaurant that employed us both shut its doors. We didn't receive any prior notification that the restaurant was closing its doors. We literally arrived ready for work, only to see it doors locked with a note stating. "Sorry for the inconveniences, but we will be closed indefinitely. Due to lack of funding, we have to shut our doors. We will notify each employee when last payment will be available." That check never made it. None of us saw our last paycheck.

Finances were growing tight, and so was Shelton's patience. He began complaining about food, lights, and anything he could think of. He had an attitude if it was too hot, or too cold. I couldn't do anything right at this point. I couldn't cook, clean, or pay bills. I was useless. I couldn't take his constant belittlement. I ended up taking a minimum wage job, working in the kitchen of a assisted living facility. It was a disgusting job, but it brought in a check. Shelton began to lighten up on busting my ass. He, not only put me down. Shelton began to be physically abusive. He'd slapped me around a few times, then he started getting aggressive. By the time we were in our third year living together we were boxing. I mean going toe to toe like Muhammad Ali, and Joe Frazier.

While working at the nursing facility I met Shelton's mom Maxine. She was a head nurse at the facility. She'd work three sixteen hour days. I'd see her one or two of her work days. She was the most beautiful soul I ever met. We'd often eat lunch together. We'd share long conversations about family, school, work...etc. Maxine was very soft spoken. Also, a fellow Virgo earth sign, just like myself. I'd lied to C for so long I almost forgot my actual birthday. What I liked most, is she didn't mind teaching me things. She helped me set up a 401k, gave advice me about setting up my very first micro savings account, introduced me to IRA's, and a few recipes. I loved Maxine as if she was my mother. I missed my mother to my core. I would never let myself mourn. I was too busy trying to survive. I cried my cries, tucked in my tail, and kept my head above water. Maxine's soft spoken demeanor was quite like my mother's.

I was five months pregnant with Shelton's son, and a nervous wreck! That's when Maxine found out Shelton was physically, and mentally abusing me. We got into a really bad fight one night while Savannah was spending the night. During the fight Shelton got so angry he threw a dresser drawer at me. The drawer hit me in the back of my legs, as I tried to run away. Savannah didn't waste any time calling Maxine, as well as her mother. It took them both all of five seconds to get to our house. Michelle stormed in screaming for her daughter. She finally found her way upstairs where Savannah, and sat on our king size bed. Michelle, barged in, grabbed Savannah with one of the meanest scowls I'd ever seen on her face. She called Shelton several trifling "mutha fucka's, he will never be shit, she didn't want Savannah seeing abuse, how he's never going to change, and so on. She vowed not to bring Savannah back until Shelton got some help for his abusive behavior. Apparently he's hit her before as well. As if her wrath through the house wasn't enough. The moment Michelle walked out the door, Maxine walked in. I swear to this very day. I think Michelle tagged Maxine, like were in tag team wrestling match. Maxine's wrath was far more worse than Michelle's. She wasn't coming up any stairs. She demanded her damn respect from the son she raised. She screamed Shelton's name with so much force, and conviction in her voice. I think she woke the ancestors. Shelton got up, and proceeded down the stairs. The afraid timid look on his face was priceless. Shelton still had three steps left to reach the bottom of the stairs. He didn't make it before Maxine grabbed him in his collar dragging Shelton down the last three. "Have you lost your goddamn mind? Where the hell do you get off hitting women? You were raised by women, and you're raising a young woman. How will you feel if you found out, some crazy ass man was hitting one of us? This is not how I raised you."

Maxine punched Shelton, in the face gut, ribs, arms. Any place she could get a clean shot at him she took it. She delivered a strong blow with every word she said.

When Maxine finally stopped beating Shelton. She turned, to face me. She looked so deep in my eyes. It was like her spirit talked to mine. It felt as though her eyes saw all of my past abuse, pain, sorrow. Most of all; Maxine knew that I lacked sense of self worth. With her eyes filled with tears, Maxine told me that she loved me, that she'd do anything in the world for me, but don't ever in a million years let her son abuse me in any way. I heard the words Maxine said to me. I simply didn't listen to the words Maxine said to me. I really do regret not listening to Maxine. Not only that but, everyone tried to warn me about being with him.

Shelton's abusive behavior was the most toxic of all. Shelton was not only abusive, and he was extremely manipulative. He'd attack the things I'm most insecure about. Then make it seem as If it was all in my head. I hated the fact that Shelton knew my secrets. The moment he'd use them against me, Iyd want all my secrets back. I was emotionally drained my entire pregnancy living with Shelton.

I endured the very same abuse I witnessed my mother, and my sisters go through. The very first man I fell in love with told me that I was worthless. My father called me stupid more than he called me by the birth name he gave me. I was caught up in an ongoing, self destructive cycle. Living a life outside of myself, always questioning my own judgement, afraid of what everyone else thought of me. Never once seeking an identity for myself. I defined myself by my relationships. This not only made me dependent on my significant other. I looked to them for validation, and reassurance... Reassurance that I was still worthy of love.

I remember when I would find out about his cheating. Shelton would beat me up for finding out! Just like my past relationship with C.

Shelton, didn't give a shit about me carrying life we created inside of me, or his daughter Savannah. Shelton abused me a few times in front of his daughter. Even while pregnant with our child. He'd even humiliate me in public.

Shelton, and I went on a dinner date with Nissa, and her fiance. We couldn't quite decide on a restaurant. My taste buds we're completely out of whack with my pregnancy. I did know for sure, that I didn't want to eat IHOP. I should've never disagreed.

Why did I say that! You would've thought I took a shit in everyone's tea.

Shelton yelled out in front of everyone.

"I don't give a fuck what you want. You are going to eat what the fuck I buy, or look stupid." Shelton began to smile at my sunken face, and demeanor. He then began to laugh as he told me. " You can get a happy meal, or starve for all I care."

I guess Shelton didn't understand that starving me, also starved his son! Most importantly; I should've never let what Shelton provided, be my resource to eat.

After our first year together, Shelton started being unfaithful, and I allowed it. I allowed myself to stay with a man that didn't respect me, or our relationship. I didn't feel myself to be worthy of love.

Years prior to Shelton, when I was just a child. My young impressionable mind believed that I was this stupid, weird, kid that couldn't do anything right.

This put a huge damper on how I chose to live my life. This unhealthy way of thinking was reflected in the type men I chose to be with. How long I stayed would depend on how convinced I was during "the honeymoon stage" This is when Shelton's manipulative behavior came in to play. He would seem so regretful, so loving. He'd take me out, buy me gifts, and lovely handbags. What I now refer to as "black eye trophies."

I allowed myself to be completely vulnerable to Shelton's honeymoon tactics, followed behind his abuse as a method to punish me.

No matter what I would go through with Shelton. I loved him like no other man before him. I even married him after giving birth to our son Emanuel. I stood tall for my marriage, and our family together.

I not only adored Shelton. I loved his family as well. I formed my own personal bond with my in-laws. Maxine made me feel like I was one of her own.

I was extremely close to Shelton's family. I felt accepted completely. No matter what Shelton, and I went through I always thought I'd be a part of the Robertson family. That was until I decided to leave. His sister Trina made sure that I knew my place. I was tolerated. The moment I decided to leave things got ugly. I was now nothing more than a "bitter black bitch." Yes, my Nubian king, so I thought. Referred to me as a "BITTER BLACK BITCH!" The went further on to say "he should've killed me, he didn't beat me with broom handles good enough, and that he didn't want to be bothered with his son. The moment I defended myself against his abusive behavior. (Not saying my measures were the most reasonable) I had to get unreasonable to do so. His sister Trina made sure to call, and tell me about myself. It was made clear to me that day, I meant nothing. When it came down to me and her brother. It would be her brother rather he's wrong, or right. This man threatened to kill me, and disowned his son. Yet I got a phone call to chastise my behavior? That was the end of my relationship with my in-laws.

I knew my relationship with Shelton was draining, often leaving me empty inside. That's where the relationship with his family came in. They would fill me up with hope.

Maxine, and I shared a beautiful mother daughter bond. A bond so strong, that I didn't know how to handle it when I lost her to cancer. Maxine was part of my earths angels, but illness cut her time on Earth short.. I have yet to grieve the loss of mother, as well as Maxine. My life has been in survival mode my entire life. I didn't have the time, or know how to grieve. No one ever asked me if I was okay. I would only be asked to perform a service. I've always been asked to perform a service of some sort. I've hardly ever been asked if I were okay. When asked I'm usually caught off guard. Not something I'm used to hearing.

After sixteen years with Shelton, and five years of marriage. I began to fall ill.

Once this happened I was no longer useful to Shelton. My body began to shut down.

I began have trouble keeping up at work. With my health declining rapidly. I could no longer depend on my body to function properly, that made me unstable for employment. My mental, and physical health began to decline right along with my marriage to Shelton.

If I asked Shelton questions about his feelings, or about him having an affair. I got my ass kicked. My life didn't matter to Shelton. My life obviously didn't mean anything to me. I allowed Shelton to treat me as if I were his doormat.

I was an emotional wreck! Not addressing any of my past trauma. Suppressing every emotion to appear strong. Truthfully, I was at the weakest point of my life. I'd lost so much with my health decline. I didn't want to loose my family too. I literally gave this man and my marriage everything I had. I fought harder for his love than I did for my life. Love is life to me.

This lead my mental state out of control. I would encounter numerous emotional breakdowns. One, after another. Fighting to make a selfish man loyal. I needed Shelton to love me as I loved him. When all along I should've loved myself enough to let go. I should've loved me more than I loved him.

The last year of my marriage I was practically begging Shelton not to give up on us, and our family. The same way I didn't give up on him.

But how? How could I expect someone to show up for me, when I never showed up for myself. I was walking, living, and breathing, pain.

Shelton started having an ongoing affair with a coworker. He already made plans to be with her, while telling me that I was over thinking as usual. He planned a life with this woman, while he was still married to me. Once the going got tough health wise. I was no longer useful in our marriage. He needed a replacement. Someone else nieve, and eager for love.

So, Shelton went out, and got himself a blonde hair, green eyed, woman. A woman that didn't care about him being another woman's husband.

Hell, who am I fooling! Shelton didn't give a shit about his own marriage. I'm not sure if he cared about anything outside of himself. He's never stood for, or fought for anything in the seventeen years I've known him.

My mental state crashed. I began to question my existence. I'd talk myself out of suicide daily, while pretending to be ok. I simply thought I'd be able to handle it. Putting on a mask daily for my children. I'm all they could depend on. Heaven forbid I fall. I thought this type of behavior was normal.

I honestly didn't understand mental illness. I thought I'd simply lived a hard life. I didn't think my feelings were out of the ordinary.

We'd often make jokes about mental illness. This wasn't something that was embraced by ethnic communities. We'd simply use the term so and so "went crazy" or simply not deal with the issue at all.

I never even thought about getting help for myself. Until the night I swallowed an entire bottle of sleeping pills.

I woke up the next day angry for being alive. I also felt like there was another purpose for my life. I survived everything meant to break me. Now, I needed help with dealing.

I found help, and started partial in patient therapy. Slowly, over some time. I began to heal. It was, and still is very challenging to break old thinking habits, and impulsive behaviors. They've been my coping mechanism my entire life. They aren't healthy, and I'm now fighting for myself. I'm fighting harder to keep my sanity, than I fought to keep any man.

I eventually filed for a divorce. Wouldn't you know Shelton didn't even bother to show up for the hearing. My divorce was granted on the evidence of domestic abuse. The courts ruled in my favor, and granted child support to be paid monthly, and reimbursement of money I paid into healthcare. Shelton was revoked all parental rights to our son Emanuel. This was due to Shelton sending over several text messages, threatening my life. He also messaged our son. Shelton wrote things to our son so inappropriate, the judge ruled it emotional abuse.

With a lack of self love, and self awareness. I allowed myself to to be a victim of abuse. I allowed myself to stay in a abusive marriage. I fought for the a man, that lied to me, cheated, and threatened to kill me.

The same man that didn't even fight for his children. I almost allowed myself to be taken out by past traumatic experiences. Over time it became natural for me to block my emotions. I based Who I was on the opinion of everyone outside of myself. Slowly losing my identity. Over time I allowed myself to become The Invisible Woman. ❁

"In a field filled with roses. I'd be the only Sunflower standing."

~Felicia Day~

The Love Letter To The Author

Dear Felicia

Felicia's love letter

Dear Felicia,

We've been together now over 40 years and I've never loved you more than I do now. Ever since that first day, I could sense that there was something special about you. We may not have been as wise to the world as we are today but I knew somehow my life was not going to be normal. Although I don't believe in a Higher Power like many We have come across, I knew that the test He had set before us would not be easy. The burden of responsibility placed upon us, the heart breaks and the loss were all part of that test. I couldn't see it then, but now I'm realizing the deeply heartfelt calluses were life given gold stars on tattered paper whose lines have been blurred for longer than you remember, but who's message speaks to a hopeful spirit that will no longer be denied.

 I'm so blessed to know you AND grow you. You are a phenomenal being with nothing else to fear and everything to gain. With that being said, I'm blocking your rear view mirror so you never have to look back, only forward as you blaze a new trail toward your dreams. So know now that through ALL times, you can count on me to push you when you're stuck, catch you when you fall, and hold you in stormy weather.

 In closing, there is nothing you can do to hurt me nor anyone else anymore. No one could ever love someone as unconditionally as I do you.

 Signed,

Your forever love,

Unapologetically Fi. 🌻 💫

Thank you.

Dedication

This book is dedicated to my unborn grandchild Peyton Skye Day. My dearest, everything I do from this day forward is to create a legacy for you. I can't wait to meet you in May. To my sons (sonshines) Joseph Day, and Samuel Robinson Jr. You both have been and always will be my inspiration to do better. There is no greater love than the love I have for you two. You both inspire me in more ways than I can count. Special thanks to John (Mr. Art International) Davison for his awesome advice, and insight. You are truly a great friend to have in my corner. To my sister from another Mister, Lisa. Baby you are one of the strongest people I know. Hell, your even stronger than you know yourself. I'm so proud to call you my friend, as well as my sister. You just light skin! Signature Health, and their staff for their endless means of support. Johnetta Ashe, my guiding star, and number one star player, Rachel McLaughlin, Tiffany Allen, Michael, Patti, Lekendra, Shelly, Lindsey, Teri, Tierra boo, Timothy Natale, and a host of other people. The team I had the pleasure of working with not only taught me coping skills needed to progress. They believed in me, and didn't give up when I almost gave up on myself. It was an absolute pleasure to work with These people. Although, I myself wasn't always cooperative. Their drive, and genuine compassion for my mental stability is what kept me fighting. These people are my heroes, and sheros. Thank you for steering me back to my life's purpose. Thank you for help in healing a tortured soul. This facility, and it's staff helped to save my life. For that I am forever grateful.

The Invisible Woman

Book Description

The story of an African American woman's struggle with physical and emotional abuse. I purposely wrote this book raw. It's written in bad Grammer,and a lot of slang. I wanted to reach women like myself. Women who are so focused on survival we forget to address our mental health. We endure so much, and the world expects us to keep going. How we sometimes let the opinion of others become the opinion of ourselves. We then get this idea that by blocking our emotions we're being strong. This story will make you question am I being resilient, or am I slowly dying? CiCi found out the hard way that a life without feeling is a life without meaning. I hope sharing my story will inspire someone to seek help. That it's ok not to have all the answers, it's ok to fall apart when life gets you down. What's not ok, is continuing to stay down once you've fallen. It's not ok to live life without purpose. To live is to love. We must first learn to love ourselves in order to live. It's ok to seek help. Most of my adult life I had to reevaluate the behaviors I was by people who didn't have their shit together. For once in my life I want to live! I will no longer be Invisible to myself. Simple me... Simply Fi.👑 🌻

"We cannot selectively numb emotions, when we numb the painful emotions, we also numb the positive emotions."

~Brene Brown~

Abuse in any form is not okay. Sometime we can be too strong for our own good.

~Felicia Day~ #MeToo